Original title:
Passion and Purpose

Editor: Jessica Elisabeth Luik
Author: Olivia Orav
ISBN HARDBACK: 978-9916-86-545-3
ISBN PAPERBACK: 978-9916-86-544-6

Undying Fire

Beneath the stars, an ember glows,
A spark that time cannot subdue.
In shadows deep, it fiercely shows,
A will that burns in every hue.

Though tempests rage and torrents fall,
The flame persists through darkest night.
Its guiding warmth, a clarion call,
A beacon pure, a source of light.

Eternal dance of flickering grace,
Against the winds, it stands unbowed.
In quiet strength, it finds its place,
Among the weary and the proud.

Forged in depths of ancient lore,
It tells of dreams that never tire.
Of trials past, and yet before,
This heart endures—undying fire.

So let it blaze within our soul,
A testament to undeterred.
For in its light, we find our whole,
In whispered flame, our truth is heard.

Soul’s Persistent Flame

In darkness where night's shadows tread,
A light persists, would not decline.
With fervent glow, it lifts its head,
A torch within, our hearts align.

Through storms and winds, it does not cease,
A beacon burning ever bright.
Amidst despair, it offers peace,
Guarding dreams throughout the night.

Its glow reflects a boundless might,
In struggles’ heart, it stands so true.
A force of nature, clear in sight,
Persisting flame, eternally blue.

Driven Essence

Where fields of hopes freshly grow,
An essence stirs with force within.
With every step, it aims to show,
The battles fought, the dreams begin.

As whispers of the dawn unfold,
A heartbeat quickens, fuels the fire.
An essence driven, brave and bold,
Chasing visions, climbing higher.

In every pulse, a rhythm strong,
It dances through the world's embrace.
With driven essence, we belong,
A testament to boundless grace.

Unmatched Ardent Will

In realms where doubt and shadows play,
An ardent will stands fierce and bright.
While others stray, it holds its way,
Guided by an inner light.

Through trials vast and waters deep,
It pierces through with endless zeal.
Its vow is one it aims to keep,
A will unmatched, none can conceal.

Within its core, a strength divine,
Foundation of unwavering might.
No challenge vast will redefine,
This ardent will, forever right.

Unbroken Strive

In fields of grey where hopes subdued,
A strive emerges, unbroken, bold.
Through paths unknown, amidst the crude,
Its journey fierce, its story told.

With footsteps firm on rugged ground,
It charts a course through thick and thin.
Unbroken strive, in echoes found,
Seeks the victory held within.

In valleys deep and peaks so high,
It's not the end that drives its quest.
An endless strive to touch the sky,
A testament to endless zest.

Undying Zeal

In the shadows where dreams abide,
A spark ignites, no force can hide.
With every breath and step I take,
A burning zeal I won't forsake.

The path is long, the night is dark,
But through the storm I'll leave a mark.
With unwavering heart and soul,
Pursuing fervor is my goal.

Beneath the weight of doubt and fear,
A steadfast light, forever near.
For in my veins ambition flows,
And with each sunrise, fervor grows.

Pure Intensity

A silent pulse, a fervent beat,
In every moment, fierce and sweet.
Through trials faced and battles won,
Intensity is never done.

The fire within, a beacon bright,
Guiding through the darkest night.
With eyes ablaze, I chase the dawn,
A passion pure, forever drawn.

Each heartbeat echoes loud and clear,
A testament to all held dear.
In every stride and every aim,
Intensity will stake its claim.

Glowing Aspirations

In twilight hours, dreams take flight,
A future painted in the night.
With hopes that gleam and hearts that dare,
Aspirations light the air.

The stars above, they gleam and guide,
A vision clear, a path so wide.
With courage firm and spirit high,
Toward the dawn, the dreams will fly.

Through valleys low and mountains steep,
A glowing heart its quest will keep.
For in each soul, a flame will burn,
And to the stars, we'll all return.

Relentless Passion

Through endless nights and tireless days,
A burning passion lights the ways.
With every step and every vow,
Relentless dreams will show us how.

The heart's desire, a force so strong,
With fervent hope, it moves along.
No barrier too great, no fear,
For with each breath, the goal is near.

In every tear and every smile,
Relentless passion makes worthwhile.
For life is lived in vivid hues,
When every moment, passion pursues.

Eternal Drive

Through valleys low and mountains steep,
A journey of unwavering will.
The path is long, the goals we keep,
Our spirits rise, our hearts fulfilled.

With every dawn, a hope renewed,
A silent vow, a promise made.
We travel light, our soul pursued,
By dreams that guide, they never fade.

The wheels of fate, they turn and spin,
On roads unknown, we boldly tread.
In every loss, a chance to win,
The fire inside, forever fed.

Unyielding Dream

In midnight's hush, it softly calls,
A dream that whispers in the night.
Through shadowed halls and empty walls,
It leads us to the morning light.

An ember born within the soul,
It flickers, dances, never dies.
No storm nor gale can make it cold,
Its truth endures beneath the skies.

Against the tide, we stand and fight,
With courage drawn from unseen streams.
To mountain's peak, through darkest night,
We chase the path of unyielding dreams.

Heart's Ambition

Beneath the stars, a silent vow,
In every beat, ambition’s tune.
The dreams we chase, they guide us now,
Their echoes bright beneath the moon.

Each step we take, a quest begun,
Our eyes set high, beyond the haze.
Through battles lost and victories won,
Our hearts ignite in fervent blaze.

With every dawn, a canvas white,
We draw our visions, bold and grand.
A journey made in endless plight,
Heart's ambition, we shall withstand.

The Inner Flame

Deep within, a flame that burns,
A light that guides through darkest night.
In every heart, a spirit yearns,
To break the chains, embrace the fight.

Through trials faced and battles fought,
The inner flame, it steers us true.
A force unseen, with fire wrought,
It leads us to the dreams we pursue.

No storm can quench this blazing core,
Nor doubts destroy its radiant gleam.
Within us burns, forever more,
The inner flame, our guiding beam.

Unquenchable Thirst

In deserts vast, I wander wide,
Beneath the sun's relentless pride,
Seeking streams in endless sway,
Oasis dreams to guide my way.

Eyes on the horizon cast,
Mirages flicker, secrets past,
Through the dunes, a path I trace,
To quench my thirst in nature's grace.

Parched and weary, onward trod,
Footprints linger, baking sod,
Hope's the compass, ever true,
Thirst for life in me renew.

Stars ignite the cooling night,
Guiding steps through twilight's light,
In the silence, whispers flow,
Quenching thirst from depths below.

Flame of Aspirations

A spark ignites within my soul,
A destined path, a burning goal,
Through trials fierce and shadows deep,
I'll chase my dreams, though mountains steep.

In the forge of hope and strife,
I'll hammer out my will in life,
With every step, a brighter blaze,
Illuminates the darkest ways.

Kindling heart with passion's fire,
I'll climb above, I'll never tire,
In pursuit of visions clear,
Each moment fuels my steadfast cheer.

A phoenix in the stormy skies,
Rise with courage, never shy,
Flame of aspirations bright,
Guides me through the longest night.

Journey of the Heart

Across the lands and seas afar,
Through twilight’s gleam and morning star,
A journey of the heart I take,
With every beat, decisions make.

Paths unknown and trails unmarked,
In depths of soul, adventures sparked,
Compass points to love and truth,
A voyage etched since tender youth.

Braving storms and basking suns,
In search of places still unsung,
Boundless skies and oceans deep,
A journey fueled by dreams in sleep.

Wanderlust that knows no bounds,
In every whisper, heart resounds,
Stepping stones and winding ways,
My heart's journey, endless days.

Eternal Ember

In the hearth of timeless flame,
Burns an ember, bright and tame,
Whispers of the ancient lore,
Tales of yore forevermore.

In ember's glow, the shadows play,
Dance of fire, night and day,
Light that never fades away,
Guiding souls along their way.

Flicker, flicker, soft and low,
In the quiet, dreams bestow,
Eternal ember, steady light,
Keeps the dark from deepest night.

Silent witness, steadfast gleam,
In the heart of every dream,
Eternal ember, ever bright,
A beacon through the endless night.

Loving Conviction

In the depths of love, a stronghold lies,
With whispers soft, and tender sighs.
A bond unbroken, ever true,
Steadfast hearts, in skies of blue.

Through storm and calm, they intertwine,
Two souls as one, in perfect line.
No force can shake, nor tear apart,
This loving conviction of the heart.

With every dawn, a promise made,
In every dusk, their fears do fade.
Hand in hand, through night and day,
In love's embrace, they find their way.

The roots grow deep, the branches spread,
Their love, a shelter overhead.
In timeless dance, they weave their fate,
A loving conviction, ever great.

Heart's Desires Unleashed

Unveil the night, where passions rise,
With stolen looks and secret sighs.
In shadows cast by moonlit beams,
Unleashed desires fill our dreams.

Through whispered winds and ember's glow,
Our hearts' desires begin to show.
Entwined in bliss, no space between,
In love's embrace, we reign supreme.

Each touch ignites a burning flame,
Both souls and spirits to proclaim.
In every breath, in every kiss,
Unleashed desires, pure and bliss.

The stars align to mark our fate,
Two hearts untamed, no need to wait.
With every beat, with every flare,
Our deepest wishes take the air.

Aroused Essence

In twilight's veil, our secrets gleam,
Two worlds collide in vivid dream.
Aroused in essence, pure and wild,
In passion's fire, hearts beguiled.

With touch so soft yet fiercely true,
Our spirits soar, as one, anew.
In every glance, in every sound,
Aroused essence, love unbound.

An arc of lightning in the night,
Embraces warm, the stars shine bright.
In realms unseen, where dreams do play,
Our love divine, in endless sway.

With every heartbeat, every sigh,
An essence aroused to touch the sky.
In love's embrace, we find our peace,
In moments shared, our hearts release.

Vibrant Pursuit

In fields of green, our spirits chase,
A vibrant world, a boundless space.
With feet that fly, and hearts that beat,
In joyous, endless pursuit, we meet.

The sun above, a guiding light,
Through day and night, love's endless flight.
In laughter's song, and whispered word,
Our vibrant dreams take wing, unheard.

Together through the paths unknown,
In every step our love has grown.
With hands entwined, pure and bright,
In vibrant pursuit, life's delight.

In every hue, in every shade,
With love's own brush, our fears we trade.
Through highs and lows, through thick and thin,
In vibrant pursuit, we always win.

Awakening Force

Morning sun breaks night's embrace,
Whispers of a brand-new phase.
Nature stirs with gentle grace,
Awakening the world's soft face.

Streams of light dance on the dew,
Colors bright and skies anew.
Birdsong tells the tales of true,
Wonders waiting, endless view.

Leaves succumb to breezes warm,
Petals bloom in perfect form.
Life resumes through calm and storm,
In the heart, an inner norm.

Mountains rise with mighty roar,
Seas unleash a storied lore.
Every heartbeat’s ancient core,
Echoes forth forevermore.

Stars above in daylight fade,
Guiding dreams that wander, laid.
Awakening force, invoke and trade,
Day anew from night parade.

Echoes of Yearning

Silent whispers in the night,
Dreams that drift beyond the light.
Hearts engage in secret flight,
Yearning gives the world its might.

Stars align in patterns old,
Stories of the heart unfold.
In the quiet, dreams retold,
Echoes sing what words withhold.

Moonbeams cast a silver hue,
Chasing shadows, hope anew.
In the dark, the spirits grew,
Yearning for a love so true.

Fields of green and skies of blue,
Paths untaken, worlds to view.
In each step, a wish construes,
Echoes of the heart ensue.

Time and space may drift apart,
Yet the yearnings fill the heart.
In each beat, a loving art,
Echoes play their timeless part.

Pursuit of Light

In the realm of fading night,
Chase the beam, pursue the light.
Hope's desire burning bright,
Lead the way, dispel the fright.

Through the maze of shadows gray,
Seeking dawn to guide our way.
Steps in rhythm, bold and gay,
Night to day, the world in play.

Glances of the golden morn,
Shaping dreams that we adorn.
In the heart, a wish reborn,
Light pursued since we were born.

Waves of color flood the skies,
Paints of dawn in lovers' eyes.
Every whisper, every sigh,
Leads us where the answers lie.

Through the night with stars as guide,
Light pursued won't be denied.
In the chase, our spirits tied,
Light within, our beacon, pride.

Inner Blaze

Deep within where shadows play,
Burns a light that guides the way.
Inner blaze that won't decay,
Casting out the doubts, dismay.

In the core, a spark ignites,
Turning dark to beacon lights.
Inner strength for endless fights,
Blaze within that always rights.

Storms may come and trials test,
Yet the blaze withstands the quest.
Every tear and heartfelt zest,
Nurtures flames that never rest.

In each heart, a fire thrives,
Fueling dreams and endless drives.
From the ashes, hope arrives,
Blaze within, our lives it strives.

Courage found in every gaze,
Strength within we daily praise.
Inner light in countless ways,
Keeps alive our endless blaze.

Roaring Intent

In shadows deep, a lion wakes,
With eyes aglow, the silence breaks,
A roar that shakes the moonlit night,
In heart of beast, a fierce delight.

With every stride, the jungle bows,
To power pure, that none allows,
The strength to conquer, never spent,
In untamed wild, a roaring intent.

The stars bear witness from above,
To primal force, and timeless love,
A guardian of the ancient grove,
Whose roar commands the winds to rove.

Through mist and dawn, the echoes fly,
An endless call, no bounds can tie,
In rhythmic beat, the night is rent,
By vivid dreams, of roaring intent.

Soul's Compass

In seas of doubt, my spirit sails,
With compass true, through storms and gales,
A guiding light before my eyes,
Where truth and hope will always rise.

Beneath the stars, my course is set,
Through trials faced, without regret,
The anchor's pull, a fleeting trial,
For paths unknown, are yet worthwhile.

The needle points to dreams long sought,
In shadows cast by fears now fought,
With faith as wind, my heart's delight,
To navigate the deepest night.

Through ebb and flow of fates unplanned,
Hands tighten on the ship's command,
The soul's compass, steady and bright,
Leads ever forth to morning's light.

Eternal Hunger

In depths unfathomed, longing grows,
A hunger deep that never slows,
Its whispers curl through nights so still,
An endless void, it seeks to fill.

Insatiable, the yearning flames,
Through countless dreams and faceless names,
A quest for more, beyond the known,
Its call, to realms where shadows roam.

No feast can quell the heart's desire,
No answer found in worldly choir,
For something vast and ever near,
This hunger feeds on hope and fear.

Through time and space, its voice will soar,
A silent urge that craves for more,
In every heart, a silent singer,
This timeless song, of eternal hunger.

Flames of Desire

In twilight's glow, where shadows play,
A spark ignites, the end of day,
With whispered breaths, the flames aspire,
To reach beyond, with fierce desire.

Their dance is wild, a passion's flight,
In curls of gold, they chase the night,
Each ember's kiss, a fervent plea,
To grasp the stars, and yet stay free.

The fire's heart, a molten core,
Of dreams entrenched, and something more,
A burning wish, unspoken yearn,
These flames consume, yet never learn.

In every blaze, a tale is spun,
Of morning's hope, and setting sun,
With incandescent dreams entire,
They rise and fall, as flames of desire.

Path of Intensity

Upon the trail where shadows wane,
Through forests thick, past silent cove,
A whisper guides with fierce refrain,
To paths unknown, yet spirits rove.

In twilight's grasp, the heart does race,
A fervent call in dawn's embrace,
With every step, we seek the grace,
In burning quest, we're set apace.

Unyielding dreams propel the stride,
Through rough terrain and turbulent tide,
Hand in hand with fate beside,
The path of fire, our strength will guide.

Each heartbeat echoes loud and clear,
In courage found, we shed all fear,
The journey's end is ever near,
With passion blazing year to year.

Along this route, where legends tread,
A fiery light is ever spread,
Intensity by purpose led,
Upon this path, we're boldly fed.

Inner Ambitions

Within the depths where visions glow,
An ember stirs, begins to spark,
Ambitions rise in steady flow,
To light the way out from the dark.

Through corridors of silent mind,
In whispered dreams, a goal we find,
A fire within, it seeks, entwined,
With every hope in heart aligned.

Beneath the surface, strength abides,
A secret force that ever guides,
In shadows deep, where fear resides,
Ambitions soar on mighty tides.

The mind's expanse, where stars collide,
A universe of will inside,
With each desire, our spirits glide,
On wings unseen, ambitions ride.

No mountain high can still the call,
No valley deep, nor ocean wall,
For inner drive shall conquer all,
As ambitions rise, we stand tall.

Faithful Expedition

Upon the sea of endless quest,
With sails unfurled to morning's light,
We venture forth at love's behest,
In faith, we soar beyond the night.

Through tempests fierce, and gales that roar,
Our heart's resolve remains secure,
In unity, we seek the shore,
Through endless dreams, our path is pure.

The stars above, a guiding beam,
With compass true, our souls redeem,
In every wave, a hopeful gleam,
On faithful seas, we chase the dream.

With every mile, our spirits grow,
In faith and trust, the winds bestow,
The strength to face what lies below,
Together through the storms we row.

To distant lands, our hearts aspire,
With faith as wind, and love as fire,
The world to see, our sole desire,
In faithful journey, we conspire.

Ignited Heartbeats

In moments paused, our hearts ignite,
A rhythm shared, in tender light,
With every beat, a love takes flight,
In synchronized and pure delight.

The pulse of life, in tandem sounds,
Through whispered nights and cherished bounds,
With each caress, our passion grounds,
In heartbeats' song, our joy resounds.

When distance calls, our pulses race,
In every thought, a warm embrace,
Across the miles, we find our place,
In heartbeats' beat, we interlace.

Our hearts, a symphony divine,
In sync, they pulse, and intertwine,
With each new dawn, our love aligns,
In rhythms deep, a sacred sign.

Forevermore, we'll share this tune,
Beneath the stars and under moon,
In heartbeats' time, our souls attune,
Eternal love, a sweet commune.

Trail of Radiance

Moonlight whispers on the glade,
Stars awaken, unafraid,
Petals silver in the night,
Guiding souls with gentle light.

Through the shadows, pathways gleam,
Wandering hearts in their dream,
Echoes of a distant song,
Lead them through where they belong.

Diamonds dot the darkened sky,
Questions asked, and no reply,
Yet the whispers hold them close,
Carrying them, a gentle dose.

Bathed in tranquil, silent grace,
Seeking love, a warm embrace,
Softly trod on sacred ground,
Radiant trails of life abound.

Night is but a fleeting veil,
Morning's glow will soon unveil,
Every step, a sacred dance,
On the trail of radiance.

Torchbearer's Path

Flames alight with fervent glare,
Paths unknown demand their share,
Guided by the burning gleam,
Chasing echoes of a dream.

Through the dark, the torch is raised,
Shadows flee where light is blazed,
Steps in rhythm, hearts attuned,
Journey made by forces hewn.

Heat and fire, trials met,
Every spark a chance beget,
Courage found in every stride,
Torchbearer's path, a faithful guide.

Through the tempest, forge ahead,
By the ember, fears are shed,
With each flicker, purpose bright,
Light infused within the night.

Endless miles, the quest persists,
Strengthened by the flame's insist,
In the glow of hope they bask,
Torchbearers fulfill their task.

Heart's Fuel

In the core, a flame resides,
Burning love, it never hides,
Passions rise and ebb anew,
Fed by dreams, the heart's true fuel.

Whispers on the midnight air,
Promises that lovers share,
Kindling sparks in twilight's theme,
Heart's bright fuel, a vivid dream.

Embers glow in soft caress,
Tender moments, truth confess,
Every beat, a fervent plea,
Boundless as the restless sea.

Yearning stirs the silent dark,
Ignite the soul, reveal the spark,
Through the haze, the fire swells,
In love's embrace, forever dwells.

Hope and longing intertwined,
Guided by the heart's design,
Fuel that blazes ever bright,
Lighting paths in deepest night.

Surge of Dreams

Waves of night in slumber swell,
Casting spells with whispered knell,
Mirrors deep of quiet streams,
Bathe the soul in surge of dreams.

Stars ignite the vast expanse,
Weaving tales of fate and chance,
Through the realms of night we soar,
Dreamscapes open, evermore.

Melodies in shadows play,
Guiding lost through astral sway,
With each pulse, the vision beams,
Rise within the surge of dreams.

Voices soft as morning dew,
Speak of futures, old and new,
Boundless lands and skies unfurled,
In the surge of dreaming world.

Gently through the curtains deep,
Carried by the dreams we keep,
In their flow, our spirits gleam,
Merging with the surge of dream.

Unseen Aspirations

In shadows deep, desires hide,
Beneath the stars, the dreams reside.
Whispers crawl, in silent night,
Hope unseen, yet burning bright.

A world unknown within the mind,
Treasures rare, we seek to find.
Through the haze they softly creep,
Echoes of what our hearts keep.

Visions form, in thoughts concealed,
Unspoken words, they soon reveal.
Flights of fancy, high and far,
Guided gently by that star.

Paths untrodden, yet to seek,
Strengths within we must not leak.
Every step in this grand flight,
Chasing shadows through the night.

Wings unseen, we soar above,
Floating on the dreams we love.
In the darkness, light will gleam,
Fueling every silent dream.

Burning Imagination

Through skies of flame, the mind does soar,
Creative sparks and something more.
In twilight realms, where shadows play,
Burning wild both night and day.

Tempest winds that stir the soul,
Dreams on fire, a vivid scroll.
Every thought a fire's spark,
Creating wonders in the dark.

Colors dance in vivid hue,
Ideas old transforming new.
From embers grow a towering blaze,
Igniting minds in endless ways.

Fuel of thought, it never ends,
Imagination's warmth extends.
Boundless, free, it knows no chains,
Burning bright through joy and pains.

In relentless fervor, it ignites,
Vision dancing with the lights.
Burning wild in endless flight,
Imagination's pure delight.

Flames of Devotion

In sacred fires our spirits blend,
No bounds our love, it does transcend.
Brighter than the midday sun,
In faith and trust, our hearts are one.

Each flicker speaks a tender truth,
Echoes of eternal youth.
In every spark, affection lies,
Flames that reach the endless skies.

A constant light in darkest night,
A beacon glowing ever bright.
No storm can douse this holy flame,
An endless dance, unyielding claim.

In reverence, our promise made,
In passion's glow, we'll never fade.
From ember small to blazing fire,
Devotion lifts us ever higher.

Together we shall rise and fall,
In love's eternal, glowing pall.
Forever bound, in flames entwined,
Burning heart and soul aligned.

Heartbeat's Quest

Through valleys deep and mountains high,
The pulse of life, it beats the sky.
Seeking truth in endless quest,
A journey's call, the heart's behest.

In every path and winding trail,
Whispers of love's soft unveil.
Steps we take with purpose clear,
Guided by what we hold dear.

From dawn's first light to twilight's end,
Memories blend and dreams ascend.
In every beat, a story's cast,
Echoes of a future vast.

Challenges rise yet hearts persist,
In every storm, in every mist.
Bold and brave, through all the strife,
Beating strong, the song of life.

With every throb, the world we seek,
A world where souls connect and speak.
In heartbeat's quest, we find our way,
Through night and into breaking day.

Embers in Motion

In the silence, flames ignite,
Echoes of the glowing night,
Swirling dance in crimson hues,
Ashen whispers mark their cruise.

Spirits rise, the shadows chase,
Through the dark, a fevered grace,
Kindling dreams we dare to hold,
Ever warm in stories told.

Mystic sparks of fleeting time,
Etched in hearts with fervent rhyme,
Flicker gently, night's devotion,
Lives we live are embers in motion.

Dreamer's Voyage

Setting sail on endless seas,
Winds of hope in gentle breeze,
Charting courses, stars align,
Dreamer's voyage through space and time.

Clouds like whispers guide the way,
Moonlit paths and break of day,
Endless quests of hearts delight,
Neon beams in silent night.

Boundless realms where dreams unfold,
Treasured tales and fortunes bold,
Each horizon is a stage,
For the dreamer's boundless voyage.

Untamed Spirit

Wild at heart, the call is clear,
Nature’s voice within we hear,
Rivers carve and mountains rise,
Untamed spirit in the skies.

Forest whispers through the leaves,
Songs of freedom, gentle pleas,
Every creature, untamed grace,
In the wild, a sacred place.

Bound by earth, yet wildly free,
Soul of fire, like the sea,
Life unbridled, passion's merit,
In each breath, the untamed spirit.

Whispers of the Heart

Softly spoken, silent schemes,
Woven threads of midnight dreams,
Love's confessions, tender art,
Carried by the whispers of the heart.

Echoes of a sweet embrace,
In the quiet, find their place,
Secret moments, soft and true,
In the chest, a love anew.

Vows unbroken, timeless hold,
Stories of the heart retold,
In each beat, a world apart,
Living through the whispers of the heart.

Radiant Drive

With dawn's first light we start anew,
On roads where hopes and dreams pursue.
Each mile a step, each turn a test,
In amber glow, we find our quest.

Beneath the sky, both vast and wide,
We chase the sun, our guide, our pride.
Through winds that whisper secrets old,
Our hearts remain, steadfast and bold.

Eyes on the horizon's beam,
In unity, like woven dream.
Mountains, valleys, rivers spanned,
By strength in numbers, hand in hand.

When weary eyes begin to close,
The stars above provide repose.
For every path, a story told,
Of Radiant Drive, both brave and bold.

At twilight's end, with journey's grace,
We rest, fulfilled, in this embrace.
A legacy of hopes revived,
In every soul, a Radiant Drive.

Burning Quest

Through shadows deep and valleys low,
A burning quest, where passions grow.
In every step, the heart ignites,
With dreams of distant, starry nights.

We climb through fears and doubts' steep crest,
Afire with purpose, never rest.
Each obstacle, a pyre's test,
In flames of will, our spirit blest.

The night may fall, the path obscure,
Yet in the dark, our flames endure.
Through storm and tempest, wind and rain,
Our fervent hearts break every chain.

Reflected in the ember's glow,
The truth of who we are will show.
With every ash, a phoenix rise,
A soul reborn beneath the skies.

For in this quest, both fierce and bright,
We find our strength in darkest night.
A legacy, where dreams beget,
The undying fire of our Burning Quest.

Celestial Ambition

In realms where stars and dreams align,
Our spirits soar, our hopes combine.
Celestial ambition lights our way,
Through endless night, to break of day.

Each constellation marks a goal,
A guiding light for every soul.
In silent whispers, they impart,
A cosmic song to courage's heart.

Across the void, we dare to leap,
Through galaxies, and space so deep.
With every breath, a vow renewed,
In cosmic dance, our fate pursued.

Bound by the light of distant spheres,
We turn away from earthly fears.
With stardust trails to guide us on,
The universe our marathon.

In every star, a dream fulfilled,
From wishes cast and courage willed.
Our legacy, a shining vision,
The endless quest of Celestial Ambition.

Inferno of Dreams

In flames of passion, dreams foretold,
An inferno, fierce and bold.
With every spark, a vision gleams,
Fuelled by our most ardent dreams.

Through trials faced, and bridges burned,
We find resolve in lessons learned.
The phoenix rise, from ash and strife,
A testament to dreams in life.

In every ember lies the might,
To turn the dark into the light.
Through every challenge, every turn,
In hearts an endless fire will burn.

The smoke may cloud, the fire may wane,
Yet dreams endure through joy and pain.
Resilient, fierce, forever bright,
Our visions climb, igniting night.

For in this blazing heart of ours,
Lie dreams that reach beyond the stars.
A legacy of hopes that gleam,
Within the perpetual Inferno of Dreams.

Consuming Vision

A future painted in shades so bright,
In dreams that kiss the starry night,
Whispers of hope in hearts ignite,
Guiding souls to take their flight.

Eyes hidden beneath veils of dreams,
Seeing the world through mystic streams,
Tearing through the silent screams,
Finding truth in moonlit beams.

Wandering thoughts in twilight's grace,
Seeking paths in a boundless space,
Echoes of a restless chase,
Longing for that tender embrace.

Candles flicker with ardent might,
In the shadows of endless plight,
Holding visions clear and tight,
Through the ever-consuming night.

A vision far and undefined,
Yet to its essence, hearts aligned,
In every breath, in every bind,
A consuming drive, untamed, unkind.

Radiant Drive

Underneath the noonday sun,
Shadows flee; the day's begun,
Chasing dreams that brightly run,
In the warmth, all fears undone.

Light pierces through the darkest night,
Giving hope, a guiding light,
With radiant drive, souls take flight,
Breaching every daunting height.

Fields of gold in endless plains,
Bound by neither walls nor chains,
Striving through the mortal pains,
Uplifted by the solar gains.

In the sparkle of morning dew,
Lives a strength that's firm and true,
A drive that casts the shadows blue,
Embracing skies of endless hue.

Through the journey, hearts will strive,
With the passion, lives revive,
In the glow where dreams arrive,
Powered by the radiant drive.

Fervent Journey

In the dawn of every day,
Whispers of a path relay,
Guiding steps along the way,
On a fervent journey's sway.

Hearts beat with relentless glee,
Through the forest, near the sea,
Seeking truths that set minds free,
Writing tales of destiny.

Mountains high and valleys low,
Every step, a tale of woe,
Stride with fervor, though winds blow,
Through the meadows, rivers flow.

Stars above in skies so wide,
Echoes of a world inside,
Along this journey, hearts collide,
Waves of time, an endless tide.

Paths unknown, yet clear as day,
In every moment, come what may,
A fervent journey lights the way,
In every night, in every ray.

Eclipsing Doubt

In the shadows, doubts reside,
Questions churn and fears abide,
Yet through the dark, our spirits bide,
Where truth and courage coincide.

Stars that flicker in the gloom,
Whispers of a brighter room,
Eclipsing doubt, the hearts consume,
In resilience, they start to bloom.

Through the veil of endless night,
Hope emerges, shining bright,
Eclipsing doubt with all its might,
Guiding us towards the light.

Eyes that search the heavens vast,
In the future find the past,
Fears that linger, fade at last,
Eclipsing doubt, shadows cast.

Burdened souls shall rise and sing,
Of the day when doubt took wing,
Hearts once chained now dance and swing,
In the freedom, echoes ring.

Renewed Spirit

With dawn's first light, the shadows flee,
A heart once weary, now set free.
The world awakens, fresh and bright,
A soul reborn in morning's light.

Each breath a promise, life anew,
The past is distant, skies are blue.
Aspiring dreams that once lay bare,
Now find their wings, soaring through air.

In every leaf, a whisper soft,
In every breeze, a spirit loft.
Nature's symphony plays its part,
Reviving joy within the heart.

With every step, the journey clear,
No longer bound by doubt or fear.
A path of light, so full of grace,
The world beyond, a vibrant space.

Embrace the change, let sorrow part,
Renewed in spirit, mind, and heart.
A tale of hope, in verses spun,
A life reimagined, just begun.

Fire in the Veins

A spark ignites within the soul,
Passion burning, forging coal.
In every beat, a rhythm wild,
A fierce desire, untamed, beguiled.

Flames dance along the heartbeat line,
An inferno, ardent, so divine.
Fueling dreams that never wane,
A fire coursing through each vein.

Through trials faced and battles fought,
A warrior's flame is never caught.
In every ember, strength is found,
A blazing spirit, unbound, unbound.

The world may try to quench the blaze,
But fire in the veins will raze.
With molten will, and eyes alight,
A force of nature in the night.

Emboldened by the fervent flame,
With every challenge, shout your name.
In burning passion, find your way,
A life's inferno, bright as day.

Sacred Devotion

In quiet moments, hearts entwine,
A pledge of love, a sacred sign.
A bond that time cannot erode,
Two spirits joined, a shared abode.

Through trials faced, and joy embraced,
In sacred devotion, hearts are traced.
A vow unbroken, strong and true,
Eternal love, in all we do.

Hand in hand, through life's great quest,
In unity, forever blessed.
With every glance, and tender touch,
A love profound, that means so much.

In whispered words, our secrets told,
In sacred trust, our hearts unfold.
Together, through both night and day,
In love, we'll always find our way.

Beneath the stars, our dreams take flight,
In sacred devotion, pure and bright.
A timeless tale, a love divine,
Forever yours, forever mine.

Infinite Drive

With eyes set high upon the peak,
A tireless will, the world to seek.
In every stride, a purpose clear,
Infinity within our sphere.

Horizons broad and dreams unbound,
In every heartbeat, strength is found.
With courage firm, we rise above,
An infinite drive, fueled by love.

Each challenge met with iron will,
A force that time cannot distill.
Through every storm, and every trial,
A relentless spirit, free of guile.

No limits hold, nor chains confine,
A destiny by our design.
With every footstep, paths are paved,
Infinite drive, forever brave.

With eyes aglow and spirits high,
We'll conquer earth, we'll touch the sky.
In every breath, our dreams alive,
A boundless heart, an infinite drive.

Journey of the Heart

Beneath the constellated sky,
A quest of love we do embark,
With every step, emotions fly,
Guided by a tender spark.

Through valleys deep and mountains high,
Our souls entwine, untouched by fear,
In laughter's echo, tearful sigh,
Together, ever drawing near.

Each path we tread, both bright and dark,
Our hearts aligned in perfect time,
Like melodies that leave their mark,
In every heartbeat, every rhyme.

With whispered hopes and dreams that soar,
We face tomorrows, hand in hand,
With love as strong as waves on shore,
Together, in a foreign land.

Beneath the stars, our spirits chart,
A journey endless, pure, and true,
In every beat, the journey's start,
Is always, endlessly, with you.

Unwavering Flame

In the shadowed night, it grows,
A flame that trembles, yet holds strong,
Through the darkest trials, it glows,
A beacon burning all night long.

Where winds may howl and waters roar,
This fire within us still prevails,
A love that time cannot ignore,
A light that never wanes or pales.

Each challenge met with steady grace,
As embers catch and hearts ignite,
In every tear and each embrace,
The flame of love, forever bright.

Through seasons change, through years unfold,
Our spirit’s warmth it shall sustain,
In tales of yore, in legends told,
The flame undying will remain.

So let the tempest rage outside,
Our flame will flicker, never tire,
In love's true glow, we will abide,
An ever-blazing heart's desire.

Boundless Drive

In every dawn, a fresh pursuit,
With courage bound and new resolve,
Our hearts as strong as ancient root,
Through life's great puzzles we evolve.

With dreams that dance upon the breeze,
And strength unyielding, fierce and wild,
We chase our goals with perfect ease,
Each challenge met with spirit's child.

In endless realms of boundless skies,
Our passions soar, unchained, untamed,
Through every fall, we rise and rise,
With fervor, fervently proclaimed.

No limits bind, nor tethered chains,
In boundless drive, we find our way,
Through joy and strife, through loss and gain,
Our hearts afire, night and day.

So let us leap, and dare, and strive,
For dreams that rest just out of sight,
In every breath, we keep alive,
Our boundless drive, our ceaseless might.

Kindling Dreams

In twilight's hush, our dreams ignite,
Soft whispers borne on evening's breath,
With every star, a guiding light,
To realms untouched by fear or death.

Through silent woods and twilight's gleam,
Our spirits soar, as if on wings,
With hopes as sweet as summer’s dream,
And joy that every vision brings.

Close your eyes and see them soar,
Beyond the clouds, beyond the night,
Where every wish and every lore,
Transforms to life, in dawn’s first light.

In each kind thought and gentle touch,
We kindle dreams in hearts that yearn,
For love and life, and hope as such,
So every spark and flame may burn.

So let these dreams, both bright and bold,
In darkness shine, in shadows gleam,
In every heart, let stories told,
Keep kindling love’s eternal dream.

Wings of Aspiration

The horizon calls with whispers low,
A beacon's light, a hidden glow,
Through storm and night, through ebb and flow,
Wings of aspiration grow.

With hearts unbound, we take the skies,
Eyes alight with dreams that rise,
Boundless hope, no dark denies,
Wings of aspiration fly.

Beyond the clouds, where eagles reign,
Through sacred winds, we break the chain,
No fear remains, no binding pain,
Wings of aspiration claim.

The future waits in shades of gold,
A story yet is left untold,
In courage cast, in daring bold,
Wings of aspiration mold.

So let us soar on hope's decree,
With open hearts, forever free,
In unity, in harmony,
Wings of aspiration see.

Guided by Fire

In the embers' glow, we find our way,
Through paths unknown, we dare to stray,
A beacon bright in night's array,
Guided by fire, we stay.

Through trials fierce, through raging storm,
In heat and light, we are reborn,
The flame within, it keeps us warm,
Guided by fire, transformed.

With every spark, a promise made,
To never let our spirit fade,
In shadows deep, our truth displayed,
Guided by fire, portrayed.

The edges blur, yet clear we see,
A future wrought in mystery,
In every blaze, in every plea,
Guided by fire, we're free.

So walk with light in darkest hour,
Embrace the strength within the fire,
In unity, our hearts inspire,
Guided by fire's eternal power.

Phoenix Rising

From ashes cold, a spark ignites,
Through darkest void, it brings the light,
A dance of flames, in bold delight,
Phoenix rising, take flight.

With wings of fire, spread wide and true,
In skies reborn, with brilliant hue,
A pledge to life, both old and new,
Phoenix rising, we too.

Through pain and loss, we're cast anew,
In tempests fierce, with strength we grew,
A journey vast, to self pursue,
Phoenix rising, renew.

In heart's embrace, we find our might,
In every dawn, a fresher sight,
A blaze of hope, in endless night,
Phoenix rising, so bright.

So rise again, with every fall,
Answer life's unyielding call,
In unity, we stand tall,
Phoenix rising, we all.

Molten Echoes

In caverns deep, where shadows creep,
The heartbeat of the earth does seep,
Through molten veins, its secrets keep,
Molten echoes, that speak and weep.

In glowing light, the stories told,
Of ancient worlds, in lava's hold,
Through time and space, a tale unfold,
Molten echoes, of ages old.

Within the core, a pulse so strong,
A rhythm born from nature's song,
In blazing dance, we move along,
Molten echoes, where we belong.

The fire's whisper, soft and low,
In tongues of flame, the legends grow,
A timeless bond, we come to know,
Molten echoes, ebb and flow.

Embrace the warmth, the earth’s embrace,
In molten light, we find our place,
A fiery path, a sacred space,
Molten echoes, in grace.

Boundless Yearning

In the night, the stars align,
Whispers curling through the pine.
Hearts with dreams, a fervent quest,
Endless paths where love is blessed.

Horizons painted with pure light,
Chasing echoes, souls in flight.
Eyes that seek where skies embrace,
Boundless yearning, time and space.

Whispers of the morning dew,
Promise of the dawn anew.
Hope and wonder finely sown,
Yearning hearts forever drawn.

Scattered wishes, cosmic thread,
Woven tales of what was said.
In yearning, we find our way,
To places dreams and love convey.

Above, the heavens brightly swirled,
A boundless yearning fills the world.
Infinite, the heart's desire,
Fuel the dreams, ignite the fire.

Driven by Fire

Flames within, a soul's desire,
Burning bright, a ceaseless fire.
Through the night, we journey far,
Guided by a radiant star.

Passion's blaze, a fierce delight,
In the darkness, gleaming light.
Driven by the fire inside,
On this path, our spirits glide.

Wisps of smoke and trails unseen,
Crafting from the heart's deep sheen.
Endless drive that fuels the flame,
In this fire, we stake our claim.

With each step, the embers grow,
Bearing light where shadows go.
Driven by a fire so pure,
Through the trials, we endure.

Emerald ash and ruby sparks,
Paint the sky when daylight darks.
Driven by a fire so grand,
We forge our dreams with steadfast hand.

Dynamic Pulse

Throbbing in the depths unknown,
A pulse dynamic, heart's own tone.
Life's rhythm in a steady beat,
Dancing through the streets' concrete.

Sunrise whispers in the dawn,
Awake, the pulse of life moves on.
With every step, the tempo grows,
In our veins, the river flows.

Vibrant hues and sounds collide,
In the pulse of life we glide.
Moments swift, the currents bind,
We move together, unconfined.

Thunderous heartbeats, cadence strong,
Bassline of our living song.
From dawn to dusk, the pulses play,
Guiding us along the way.

Through the echoes in the night,
Dynamic pulse, a constant light.
Feel the surge, the world within,
In this beat, we all begin.

Fire of the Soul

Deep within, where shadows play,
Fire of the soul holds sway.
Igniting dreams in quiet hours,
Fueling life with unseen powers.

Glimmers in the eyes so bright,
Mirrors of a spirit's light.
Through the ashes, rise anew,
In the soul, the fire true.

Boundless as the open sea,
Soul's fire burns eternally.
With each breath, the flames aspire,
Higher still, our hearts' desire.

In the silence, whispers call,
Echoes from the fire's thrall.
Passions forged by flames conspire,
In the dance of soul's own fire.

Light the path where shadows roam,
Fire of the soul, guiding home.
Through the night and into day,
Within us, the flames hold sway.

Vision's Embrace

In dreams where shadows gently play,
A silent muse begins to trace,
The hues of dawn in soft array,
Enfolded in a vision's grace.

Through whispers of a twilight breeze,
Aspiring stars begin to dance,
In lofty dreams they find release,
Their light, a hopeful, bright expanse.

A future painted in the skies,
With brushes made of golden light,
Drawn deeply with enchanted sighs,
A world reborn, anew in sight.

In every corner of the night,
The echoes of tomorrow wait,
A canvas spun in silver light,
Where dreams and destiny relate.

Embrace the visions as they come,
Let shadows guide through realms unknown,
For in the quiet, hearts become,
A constellation of their own.

Unquenchable Fire

Beneath the starlit evening's veil,
A spark begins to flicker slow,
Within the heart it tells a tale,
Of flames that surge and brightly glow.

Through tempests fierce and waters wild,
The fire persists, unwavering,
A beacon for the lost, reviled,
In warmth, forever savoring.

Against the dark, it battles through,
A phoenix rising from the ash,
Its fervor strong, its light anew,
No storm could force its fire to crash.

The embers dance in fervent glee,
While shadows flee in wild dismay,
For love and hope ignite the key,
That keeps despair at bay, away.

Unquenchable, it roars and sings,
This fire of undying might,
Endure it shall, through all things,
A torch that fills the endless night.

Resilient Pulse

A heart beats strong beneath the tide,
Resilient through each storm and strain,
With every throb, a surge of pride,
Against the odds, it feels no pain.

Through corridors of time and space,
Its rhythm never weakens, slows,
In every trial it finds grace,
And through each trial, stronger grows.

Amidst the chaos and the noise,
It holds firm to its steady beat,
With steadfast calm, it yet enjoys,
The harmony where life and spirit meet.

The world may turn and twist its path,
Yet pulse remains, a constant guide,
Through light and shadow, love, and wrath,
In persevering stride, it will abide.

Resilient pulse, enduring soul,
A beacon in the darkest night,
Together, hearts will make us whole,
With beating strength through endless fight.

Searing Focus

In the chaos of a crowded scene,
A single thought burns clear and bright,
With eyes that pierce the smoky sheen,
And searing focus as its light.

Through tangled webs of fear and doubt,
A path emerges pure and true,
Unyielding to the twisted route,
Its flame illuminates the view.

With every breath, the vision grows,
A singular resolve takes hold,
Against the tempest fiercely blows,
Unmoved by falsehoods, firm and bold.

In every challenge stands a chance,
To sharpen, hone the keenest edge,
It carves the path in onward stance,
With focus, clear, it makes its pledge.

Searing focus, undeterred,
In clarity, it finds its way,
With purpose and with strength conferred,
It leads through night into the day.

Quest for Meaning

Beneath the arch of ancient skies,
I wander through the twilight's gleam,
In search of truth where silence lies,
And whispers float within a dream.

Through forests deep and mountains high,
The river's song, a cryptic guide,
With every step, I seek to find,
The hidden realm where secrets hide.

In shadows cast by moonlight's grace,
Unveiling realms of yore untold,
The quest for meaning finds its place,
Within the heart, both brave and bold.

Eclipsing fears of the unknown,
Where mortal steps have dared to tread,
In journeys where the soul has grown,
From ashes where the dreams are fed.

And in the end, beneath the stars,
The quest unfolds a mystic beam,
For all we seek is never far,
When we embrace the waking dream.

Silent Determination

In quiet hours before the dawn,
A steadfast heart begins its stride,
Against the odds, its will is drawn,
To shores where aspirations bide.

No raucous cheer or blaring horn,
No need for grand, resounding praise,
In silence, strength and hope are born,
With every step, new paths it lays.

Through trials carved by unseen hands,
And shadows cast on verdant fields,
Its silent roar in lieu of grand,
Reveals the strength true courage yields.

Though silent as the midnight rays,
Its echoes stretch beyond the veil,
The quiet force in all its ways,
No storm or gale could render frail.

For in the stillness of the night,
Determination's voice is clear,
A guiding star, both calm and bright,
That paves the road despite the fear.

Boundless Zeal

With fervent heart and eyes aglow,
We chase the dreams within our sight,
Through fields of green and fields of snow,
Our zeal, a beacon in the night.

No mountain tall, no ocean wide,
Can dampen spirits strong and free,
For in each step, our hearts confide,
A passion fierce, destiny.

Through stormy seas and desert sands,
Our zeal persists, unfazed by plight,
With every breath, with willing hands,
We shape our legacy in light.

A fire within, it lights our path,
And ever forward, we shall stride,
Against all odds, in joy and wrath,
Our boundless zeal shall be our guide.

Together in this journey vast,
With hearts as one, with spirits high,
Our boundless zeal forever lasts,
As we embrace the endless sky.

Path of the Spirit

Along the path where shadows play,
A spirit treads with gentle grace,
Through mystic realms, both night and day,
In search of wisdom's warm embrace.

The wind, a whisper soft and kind,
Guides footsteps through the silent trees,
Where ancient truths, by heart, aligned,
Unveil their secrets on the breeze.

Each step a beat in nature's song,
Syncopates with the cosmic rhythm,
Within such harmony, we long,
For unity with all within.

No mortal bounds or earthly chains,
Can hold the spirit's questing stride,
For in its essence, it remains,
A wanderer through time and tide.

And as the path unfolds its light,
Through realms unseen by human eyes,
The spirit's journey, ever bright,
Ascends to where the boundless lies.

Fire Within

In shadows deep, a spark ignites,
Whispering dreams, in moonlit nights.
A flame that dances, fierce and thin,
Breathes life into the fire within.

Through storm and gale, it fiercely burns,
A beacon bright, with every turn.
No fear or doubt, no dark chagrin,
Can quench the light of fire within.

Embers glow with passion's heat,
A dance of life, both wild and sweet.
In every heart, it's always been,
The unstoppable fire within.

Courageous hearts, with spirits keen,
Embrace the force, unseen, serene.
In silent strength, they bravely spin,
Fueled by the fierce fire within.

As dawn breaks forth, the world anew,
The fire within will see them through.
With steadfast hearts, they rise, they win,
Unleashing the power of fire within.

Driven by Stars

Beneath the sky, where dreams are spun,
Chasing the light of the midnight sun.
A journey paths where hope embarks,
Guided always, driven by stars.

Dreamers roam with eyes aglow,
Through velvet nights, on winds they flow.
Each step, a story, each breath, a farce,
In realms unknown, driven by stars.

Past shadows cast, the light aligns,
Unveiling truths, of ancient signs.
In cosmic dance, with fervent hearts,
Their course remains, driven by stars.

Whispers of time and endless space,
Embrace the ones who dare the chase.
Beyond the veil, where nothing mars,
Their fate is sealed, driven by stars.

With every dawn, and dusk's embrace,
They find their peace, in endless grace.
For in their souls, no fate ajar,
So long as they are driven by stars.

Heartbeat of the Soul

In quiet moments, soft and still,
A whisper speaks, a gentle thrill.
A rhythm pure, that takes control,
The timeless beat, the soul's own goal.

Each breath we take, each step we tread,
Resonates within, a thread.
A symphony that makes us whole,
The steady pulse, the heartbeat of the soul.

Through joy and sorrow, pain and grace,
It never ends, this sacred trace.
In silence deep, we find the role,
To listen to the heartbeat of the soul.

Beneath the noise, in life's embrace,
A quiet hum, a hidden space.
Where our true selves, our spirits, stroll,
To the constant heartbeat of the soul.

And as we journey, paths unfold,
With hearts entwined, both young and old.
We seek the truth, the ultimate goal,
In listening to the heartbeat of the soul.

Relentless Zeal

Through trials faced, with courage steeled,
Their strength unseen, a force revealed.
With hearts afire and eyes that feel,
They charge ahead with relentless zeal.

No mount too high, no sea too wide,
Their spirits soar, with every stride.
In every wound, their strength does heal,
They rise again with relentless zeal.

Where others falter, they prevail,
With every breath, they tell the tale.
A journey bold, where dreams congeal,
Forged in the fire of relentless zeal.

Night and day, the quest unfolds,
With passion pure, and hearts so bold.
Unyielding force, they cannot kneel,
They press on with relentless zeal.

The path is long, the end unknown,
Yet in their hearts, the seed is sown.
For dreams achieved, and hopes they seal,
Are bred within such relentless zeal.

Burning Aspirations

In the heart where dreams ignite,
Fires blaze through endless night,
Glimmers chase the dark away,
Fuels a vision, bold and bright.

Rising flames of passion grand,
Spread their glow across the land,
With each ember's fervent call,
Hope and future hand in hand.

Phoenix from the ash takes flight,
Breathes in strength, exhales pure might,
Forges paths where none exist,
Soars aloft in new daylight.

Yearning lights the ember's glow,
Whispers secrets we all know,
In the crucible of dreams,
Seeds of destiny do grow.

Fire within the soul does burn,
Lessons learned with each return,
Paths that challenge, roads untried,
Guide us as our spirits yearn.

Torrent of Ardent Will

Mighty river, fierce and swift,
Over boulders, endless drift,
Carves its channel deep and strong,
Turns to gold each simple rift.

Rushing waters of desire,
Fueling hearts that never tire,
Unstoppable, fierce and true,
Sets the soul’s resolve on fire.

In the torrent, dreams cascade,
Bringing forth what will not fade,
Sweeping past the doubts and fears,
In its wake, foundations laid.

Waves of courage, tides of love,
Guide the spirit from above,
With each pulse, resolve renewed,
Purpose beckons hand in glove.

Flowing onward, destiny's stream,
Carries forth our inner gleam,
Nature's force and human will,
Crafts the echoes of our dream.

Lustrous Yearning

Stars above, a gleaming light,
Calling through the endless night,
Wishes formed in silent prayer,
To the heights where dreams take flight.

In each sparkle, boundless hope,
Golden threads with which we cope,
Weaving tales of future fair,
With a silvered, starry rope.

Hearts aglow, a glowing fire,
Fanning flames of pure desire,
Chasing shadows from our mind,
Lifting spirits ever higher.

Dreams of brilliance, shine so bright,
Through the darkness, purest light,
Beckons us to journey far,
To the morning from the night.

Hope immortal, ever gleams,
In the tapestry of dreams,
Lighting paths with yearning's flame,
Guides us to our fullest themes.

Spirit's Quest

Uncharted roads and unseen lands,
Beckon forth from ancient sands,
Spirit rises with the dawn,
Guided by unseen hands.

Journey's call through realms untold,
Hearken spirits brave and bold,
Wisdom gathered, truths revealed,
Courage in each step enrolled.

Through the valleys, over peaks,
In each whisper, destiny speaks,
Footsteps echo in the glen,
Every path a story seeks.

Hearts aligned with questing soul,
Find in journey, self and goal,
Every trial a lesson learned,
Every part its precious whole.

In the journey, spirit grows,
Through each challenge, essence knows,
Quest of life, so richly blessed,
By the path where purpose flows.

Fervent Journey

Through winding paths and ardent streams,
We chase the light of distant dreams.
In shadows cast, our spirits soar,
To find what fate and time restore.

Each step, a whisper of the past,
An echo of a love to last.
With hearts aflame, we march ahead,
To realms where only hope is led.

In twilight hues, our souls ignite,
A beacon through the darkest night.
With every dawn, we greet anew,
The fervent journey we pursue.

No storm shall break our boldest stride,
Across the ever-changing tide.
For in our hearts, a blazing truth,
We seek the flame of endless youth.

United in this quest we stand,
Embracing life with open hand.
Through joy and pain, our spirits fuse,
To find the path that we shall choose.

Life's True Calling

In whispers soft, the morning breaks,
A truth within, the soul awakes.
With every breath, we seek the call,
To find the place where we belong.

Amidst the noise, the silent plea,
To live with purpose, wild and free.
With heart and mind in perfect tune,
We chase the call beneath the moon.

Through trials faced and mountains high,
We lift our gaze towards the sky.
For in the quest, we find our name,
A beacon lit by passion's flame.

In every task, a chance to grow,
To glean the seeds that life bestows.
With open arms and open heart,
We grasp the chance for a new start.

In unity, we forge ahead,
To where our deepest dreams are led.
For in the journey, we shall find,
Life’s true calling, intertwined.

Burning Resolve

With steady gaze and purpose clear,
We stand against the tide of fear.
In burning resolve, our spirits rise,
To conquer doubt and break the ties.

Each challenge faced is but a test,
To push us forward, to our best.
In shadows deep, a flame will glow,
Of strength that only time will show.

Through night and storm, we hold the fire,
To climb the peaks, to lift us higher.
In moments dark, we find the light,
A beacon in the endless night.

With every fall, we rise again,
To face the world, amid the pain.
For deep within, a fire burns,
A lesson that the spirit learns.

United in this burning quest,
We find the courage to invest.
For in our souls, the embers bright,
Of burning resolve, to win the fight.

Fiery Endeavors

In flames of red and gold we strive,
Through endless nights, our dreams alive.
With passion's fire, we blaze the trail,
In fierce pursuit, we shall not fail.

Through every storm, our spirits burn,
In every heart, the flames will churn.
With eyes alight and purpose clear,
We face the world, with naught to fear.

In unity, we forge our fate,
Through trials faced and opened gate.
With every spark, our strength renewed,
In fiery endeavors, dreams pursued.

From ashes rise, the phoenix cries,
In endless sky, where freedom lies.
With wings of fire, we soar and glide,
In search of truth we cannot hide.

Together in this quest we stand,
With blazing hearts and open hand.
For in the fire, we find our might,
In fiery endeavors, we ignite.

Soulful Journey

Through winding paths where shadows play,
Our spirits seek the light of day.
With every step, a quest unfurls,
To find the heart within our world.

Beneath the sky, so vast and wide,
We chase the dreams we hold inside.
The stars above, a guiding glow,
Illuminate the paths we know.

Across the lands of time and space,
We follow trails that leave no trace.
In whispered winds, the truth we'll hear,
A soulful journey brave and clear.

Through valleys deep and mountains tall,
We answer to the spirit's call.
For in the depths of soul's embrace,
We find our home, our sacred place.

The journey's end, a circle spins,
Returning where the soul begins.
In every step, a lesson learned,
A soulful journey, heart discerned.

Relentless Fervor

In fires that burn with endless might,
We forge our dreams in darkest night.
With passion's blaze, we carve our way,
Relentless fervor, come what may.

Through storm and gale, we stand upright,
Our spirits strong, our hearts ignite.
With every beat, we push ahead,
Unyielding dreams that won't be dead.

Against the odds, through trials vast,
We chase the dawn, we hold steadfast.
With fervor fierce, we will transcend,
A legacy that knows no end.

In battles fought with fervent zeal,
Our inner strength becomes our shield.
Relentless force within us lies,
To conquer all and touch the skies.

The fervor drives us ever on,
To see the rise of hopeful dawn.
With hearts aflame and spirits high,
Relentless fervor won't deny.

Deepest Drive

In caverns of the soul so deep,
Where hidden truths and secrets sleep.
We seek the spark that keeps alive,
The core within, our deepest drive.

Through silent depths, where shadows rest,
We find the strength within our chest.
No fear can halt, no doubt can bind,
The power of the driven mind.

In quiet moments, still and clear,
We touch the pulse of what we bear.
Our deepest drive, a force unseen,
Propels us toward our truest dreams.

With every challenge, every trial,
We rise again, we find our style.
For in our hearts, the fervor thrives,
The essence of our deepest drives.

Through life's vast sea, we navigate,
Our inner fire will not abate.
With courage strong and spirits high,
Our deepest drives will never die.

Vortex of Ambition

In swirling winds of fervent dreams,
We cast our hopes like beams of light.
Through shadows thick and silent screams,
Ambition turns the darkest night.

The path, a spiral carved in time,
Where whispers guide and stars align.
Each step, a pulse, a beating rhyme,
Propelling forth what we design.

With hearts ablaze in fire's embrace,
We chase the dawn, though skies may tear.
For in the storm, we find our place,
Driven by a will so rare.

Embers rise in twilight's kiss,
A dance of power and intent.
Into the vortex's abyss,
Our spirits soar, our dreams unbent.

Through tempests wild and unseen force,
We harness hope, we chart our course.

Core of Brilliance

In quiet depths where whispers sing,
A spark ignites the shadowed night.
From mystery, pure light takes wing,
Revealing truth with gentle might.

Within the heart's unwavering glow,
Lies brilliance, vast and unconfined.
A beacon in the ebb and flow,
Of thoughts profound and undefined.

Ideas bloom in silent grace,
Expressions raw, yet finely spun.
Illuminating every space,
With wisdom's guide for everyone.

Through trials fierce, in darkest times,
Its radiance never wanes or flees.
But shines as gentle, guiding chimes,
Unlocking minds with crafted keys.

At the core, where essence thrives,
Brilliance lives, and hope arrives.

Soul's Pursuit

In realms where shadows softly merge,
A quest begins in silent hues.
The soul embarks on currents' surge,
Seeking truths, where none refuse.

A journey through the boundless night,
Where echoes of the past entwine.
Each footfall, a spark of light,
Revealing paths both vast and fine.

The heart, a compass through the storm,
Guides the weary, restless mind.
In search of warmth, a place to form,
The ties that destiny will bind.

Through trials faced with valor's grace,
And whispers of what might become.
The soul pursues, an endless chase,
Toward the beat of life's own drum.

In every step, a piece revealed,
The deeper echoes, gently healed.

Relentless Journey

Through valleys deep and mountains high,
We tread with hearts both bold and pure.
In rain-soaked lands and sunburnt sky,
The path remains, though unclear.

Strength in every forward stride,
Resilience marks each breath we take.
No turning back, no place to hide,
Our courage sets the skies awake.

Across the seas of endless dreams,
Through tempests wild and trials faced.
In every stream, and winding seams,
The journey's call is deeply traced.

We press beyond the veils unseen,
Where shadows dance and fears give chase.
In endless night, through morn serene,
With spirits high, we keep our pace.

The journey's song, a ceaseless tune,
Relentless hearts, forever immune.

Heart's Fierce Flame

In the night, the stars ignite,
A passion burning, pure, and bright.
The heart's fierce flame shall never die,
A beacon in the endless sky.

Through storm and calm, it softly glows,
A light that every soul soon knows.
A dance of fire within the chest,
A love that never finds its rest.

In whispered dreams, it softly sings,
Of boundless, uncharted things.
Each heartbeat, a drum, a wild claim,
To fuel the heart's fierce, fervent flame.

With every beat, the world anew,
A pulse of promise, strong and true.
No shadows dim, no sorrows tame,
The heart's undying, fierce flame.

A blaze that climbs and never drains,
Of tears and joys, through loss and gains.
In this eternal, burning game,
Lives on, the heart's fierce, timeless flame.

Resilient Quest

Upon the path, through wind and rain,
A resilient quest, through joy and pain.
In every step, a hope renewed,
A dream pursued, a life reviewed.

With courage, strength, we forge ahead,
Though doubts and fears may fill our head.
The quest for truth, for love, for peace,
A journey that shall never cease.

In valleys low, on mountains high,
With will unbent, beneath the sky.
Each challenge met, a step profound,
Resilient quest, where dreams are found.

Through darkest night and brightest day,
We find our path, we make our way.
With hearts unyielding, spirits strong,
The journey's end where we belong.

For in this quest, we find our truth,
In ageless wisdom, in eternal youth.
Resilient quest, through ebb and flow,
Our hearts and souls will always grow.

Blazing Silence

In the quiet of the night,
A blazing silence, pure and bright.
No words are said, yet all is heard,
In whispered thoughts, without a word.

A fire burns within the hush,
A roaring flame within the crush.
In solitude, a world unfurls,
In silence, life's great symphony twirls.

The stars above, they softly gleam,
In blazing silence, like a dream.
A cosmic dance of light and shade,
In stillness, all of life portrayed.

Through silence, hearts connect as one,
In unison, as the world is spun.
A bond unspoken, deep and true,
In blazing silence, me and you.

The quiet speaks, the stillness sings,
Of endless nights and timeless springs.
Within this calm, a fire's embrace,
A blazing silence, full of grace.

Devoted to the Dream

In sleep's embrace, the visions rise,
A world unfolds before our eyes.
Devoted to the dream's sweet call,
Where endless possibilities enthrall.

With every breath, a story spins,
In dreams, our true life begins.
A canvas vast of hopes and fears,
A tapestry of smiles and tears.

In twilight's realm, we find our peace,
A haven where all struggles cease.
Devoted to the dream's pure light,
We journey through the endless night.

With hearts that yearn and souls that soar,
We seek a world worth fighting for.
In dreams, we find the strength to climb,
To conquer space, to vanquish time.

For in the dream, we are complete,
Where every challenge, we can beat.
Devoted to our sacred gleam,
We live and love, devoted to the dream.

Printed in the USA
CPSIA information can be obtained
at www.ICGtesting.com
LVHW050728010824
787081LV00003B/27

9 789916 865453